D1093233

Searchlight
BOOKS™

Do You Dig
Earth Science?

Marveling at
Minerals

Sally M. Walker

Lerner Publications Company
Minneapolis

Lerner Publications Company
A division of Lerner Publishing Group, Inc.
241 First Avenue North
Minneapolis, MN 55401 U.S.A.

Website address: www.lernerbooks.com

Library of Congress Cataloging-in-Publication Data

Walker, Sally M.
    Marveling at Minerals / by Sally M. Walker.
        p.   cm. — (Searchlight books™—Do you dig earth science?)
    Audience: 8–11
    Includes index.
    ISBN 978–1–4677–0022–1 (lib. bdg. : alk. paper)
    1. Minerals—Juvenile literature. 2. Rocks—Juvenile literature. 3. Mineralogy—
Juvenile literature. I. Title.
    QE365.2.W352 2013
    549—dc23   2012010392

Manufactured in the United States of America
1 – PC – 12/31/12

Contents

Chapter 1

WHAT IS A MINERAL?

Minerals are amazing.
We use them to build houses.
We use them to make jewelry.
We even write with a mineral. But
what is a mineral?

We use minerals to write.
How else do we use
minerals?

A mineral is a substance found in nature. Minerals are solid. They are not alive, like plants and animals are. Earth has more than thirty-five hundred different kinds of minerals.

THIS MINERAL IS CALLED GRAPHITE. GRAPHITE IS USED IN PENCILS.

Atoms

Minerals are made of atoms. Everything in the world is made of atoms. Atoms make up trees, clouds, rocks, books, and you. Atoms are very tiny. Billions of atoms could fit on the dot over the letter *i*. There are many different kinds of atoms.

Atoms make up rocks such as these.

Some minerals are made of only one kind of atom. Gold is a mineral made only of gold atoms. Another mineral, called silver, is made only of silver atoms.

Only one kind of atom is in this piece of gold.

Most minerals are made of two or more kinds of atoms. Some atoms pull on one another. When they do, the atoms can bond. Bonding is joining together. A mineral forms when certain atoms bond. Bonding holds the atoms tightly together.

This mineral is called calcite. It is made of three kinds of atoms.

A mineral called halite is made from atoms called chlorine and sodium. Halite is found in many places. Most people call halite by another name. They call it salt!

This is halite. Halite is salt.
You might find it on your kitchen table.

Graphite and diamond are minerals. Both graphite and diamond are made only of carbon atoms. But graphite and diamond look nothing alike. Why don't graphite and diamond look alike?

Graphite and diamond don't look alike because their atoms are arranged in different ways. The atoms inside each mineral are packed together in a certain way. Every mineral has its own special arrangement of atoms.

The mineral on the left is graphite. The mineral on the right is diamond.

In graphite, the carbon atoms are arranged in flat sheets. The sheets can break apart easily. This makes graphite soft.

In diamond, the carbon atoms are arranged in a way that makes them stay tightly together. This makes diamond hard.

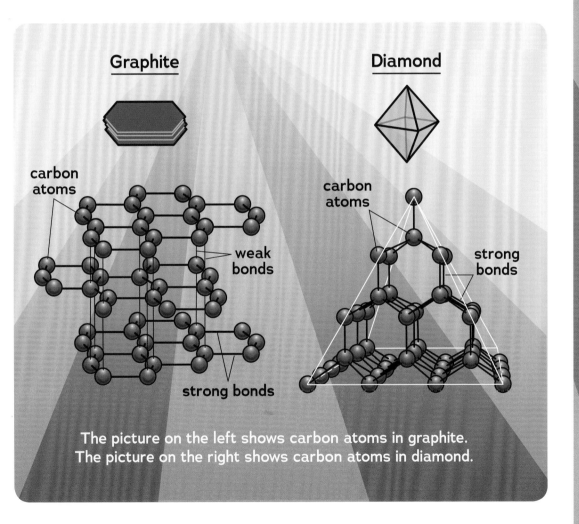

Graphite

Diamond

carbon atoms

weak bonds

strong bonds

carbon atoms

strong bonds

The picture on the left shows carbon atoms in graphite.
The picture on the right shows carbon atoms in diamond.

Crystals

A mineral's atoms can make shapes called crystals. A crystal gets its shape from the way the atoms inside it are arranged. Crystals have smooth, flat surfaces and sharp edges.

Crystals can be many different shapes. Some crystals are long and have pointed ends. Others are shaped like cubes.

These crystals have long shapes.

Crystals need room to grow. Crystals can become very big if they have lots of open space to grow. Crystals can grow even bigger than you!

But most crystals stay small. They don't have enough room to grow big. Sometimes many crystals are packed tightly together. The flat surfaces squeeze into one another. You cannot see the different crystals anymore.

These crystals have grown very big.

Chapter 2

DESCRIBING MINERALS

Minerals come in many different colors. They can be hard or soft. They can be many shapes and sizes. Describing minerals helps us to identify them.

This piece of quartz looks pink. But quartz is not always pink. Do you know why?

Describing a mineral's color may be easy. But color is not the best way to identify a mineral. A mineral may not always have the same color. Sometimes different atoms get trapped inside a mineral when it forms. These different atoms can change the color of the mineral.

THIS PIECE OF QUARTZ HAS A GRAYISH COLOR.

How Hard Is That Mineral?

A better way to describe a mineral is by testing its hardness. Some minerals are very soft. One soft mineral is called talc. A person's fingernail can scratch talc.

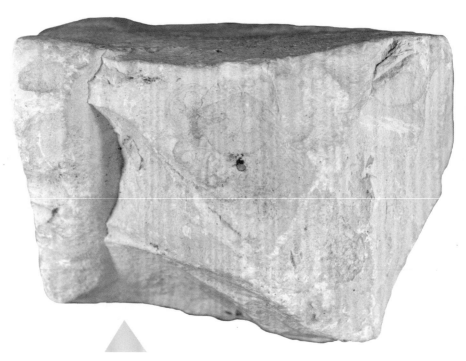

TALC IS A SOFT
MINERAL.

Diamonds are the hardest mineral. A diamond can scratch glass.

Other minerals are hard. Quartz is much harder than talc. A metal nail is not hard enough to scratch quartz. But a diamond can scratch quartz. Diamond is the hardest mineral of all.

A Mineral Scale

Scientists compare the hardness of different minerals. They use a special scale. This scale gives numbers to minerals. Soft minerals have low numbers. Hard minerals have high numbers. Hard minerals can scratch soft minerals. The higher a mineral's number is, the more minerals it can scratch.

MOHS' SCALE		HARDNESS OF OTHER ITEMS	
Hardness	Mineral	Hardness	Item
1	Talcum powder		
2	Gypsum	2.5	Fingernail
3	Calcite		
4	Fluorite	3	Penny
5	Apatite		
6	Orthoclase	4–5	Iron nail
7	Quartz		
8	Topaz	5.5	Kitchen knife blade
9	Corundum		
10	Diamond		

Scientists use a scale for measuring minerals' hardness. It is called Mohs' scale. The chart on the left is Mohs' scale. The chart on the right shows the hardness of some other items.

Streak Plates

A tool called a streak plate also helps us to study minerals. A streak plate is made of white tile. People scrape minerals across streak plates. Some of the minerals make colored lines on the plates. Different minerals make lines that are different colors. The lines are tiny bits that have scraped off the minerals. A mineral called hematite makes a reddish-brown streak. The mineral quartz makes a white streak.

Streak plates such as this help us to study minerals.

How Does It Break?

Some minerals break apart in a special way. The broken edges have smooth, flat surfaces. The arrangement of the minerals' atoms makes them break this way. Mica is a mineral that breaks apart in flat surfaces. A person can pull mica apart into very thin sheets. Mica is easy to identify by the way it breaks.

Mica breaks apart in flat surfaces.

Halite and galena can be identified by the ways they break too. They break smoothly in more than one direction. Their flat, broken edges make pieces shaped like cubes.

GALENA BREAKS SMOOTHLY
IN MORE THAN ONE
DIRECTION.

Sparkly, Shiny, Oily, or Dull?

The way a mineral's surface looks helps scientists to identify it. Light makes a diamond's flat surfaces sparkle brightly, like glass. Some minerals look like shiny metal.

This mineral is galena. Its surface shines like metal.

Some minerals look as if they have oil on their surfaces. Other minerals look dull. Their surfaces do not shine.

This mineral is turquoise. It has an oily surface.

Chapter 3

HOW DO MINERALS BECOME ROCKS?

Earth's minerals are very important. When the minerals mix together, they become rocks. Rocks are everywhere on Earth.

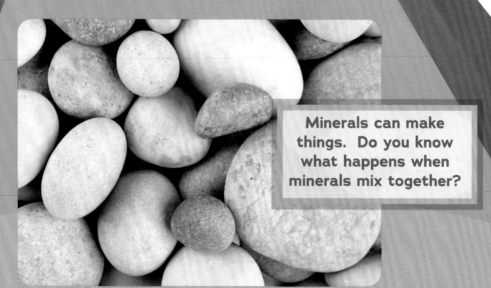

Minerals can make things. Do you know what happens when minerals mix together?

Chains of rocky mountains rise above Earth's surface. Melted rocks are deep inside Earth. But how do minerals become rocks?

Rocks are everywhere on Earth.

Melting and Cooling

It is very hot deep inside Earth. It is so hot that rocks melt. Melted rock inside Earth is called magma. Magma is made of many minerals. As magma cools, the minerals harden together and become rock. Rocks made from cooled magma are called igneous rocks.

THESE IGNEOUS ROCKS ARE MADE
FROM COOLED MAGMA.

Granite is an igneous rock. Granite contains the minerals quartz, feldspar, and mica. Gray-colored crystals in granite are quartz. Pink crystals are feldspar. Mica crystals can be black or gray.

Can you see the quartz, feldspar, and mica inside this piece of granite?

Heat and Squeezing

Earth has an outer layer called the crust. Earth's crust is very heavy. It presses down on rock that is under it. The pressing can make heat. Heat and squeezing changes rocks. Rocks changed by heat and squeezing are called metamorphic rocks.

Heating and squeezing created this metamorphic rock.

Gneiss is one kind of metamorphic rock. Gneiss forms when the minerals in a piece of granite are squeezed and heated. The squeezing and heat make the mineral's atoms line up. The atoms become layers of different colors.

Can you see the layers of color in this piece of gneiss?

Dissolving and Cementing

Water dissolves some minerals. Water with dissolved minerals in it flows under the ground. The dissolved minerals fill tiny spaces between bits of mud, sand, stone, shell, and bone. Bits of mud, sand, stone, shell, or bone are called sediments. The minerals cement the sediments together. Cementing is gluing together. The cemented sediments become a kind of rock called sedimentary rock.

Cemented sediments make up this sedimentary rock.

Limestone is a sedimentary rock. Limestone is formed when water that contains the mineral calcite surrounds sediments. The calcite cements the sediments together. They become limestone.

Limestone is made of sediments. It is a sedimentary rock.

Chapter 4

HOW DO PEOPLE USE MINERALS?

People use minerals in many ways. We grind a mineral called gypsum into a powder. The powder is mixed with liquid. Then it is made into flat, solid sheets. The sheets are used as walls in homes and other buildings.

This is a gypsum sheet. It is made of a mineral called gypsum. Do you know how we use gypsum sheets?

Toothpaste contains a mineral called fluorite. Fluorite helps to keep your teeth healthy and clean.

Fluorite in toothpaste helps keep your teeth healthy.

Some minerals can be made into metals. Copper is a metal that is made from a mineral. Some wire is made out of copper. The electricity in our homes, schools, and offices often flows through copper wires.

Electricity often flows through copper wires such as these.

The mineral bauxite is made into a metal called aluminum. We use aluminum to make the frames of windows and doors. Aluminum baseball bats are made from bauxite too.

This baseball bat contains the mineral bauxite.

The mineral titanium may have helped to decorate your home. Titanium gives a white color to some paints, paper, and plastic materials.

White paint often contains the mineral titanium.

Minerals All Around

Minerals are an important part of Earth. They are the ingredients needed to make rock. They are useful for making things.

Minerals are beautiful to look at. You may be surprised by how many minerals you see every day. What minerals can you find where you live?

Many minerals are very beautiful.

Glossary

atom: a tiny particle. Everything in the world is made of atoms.

bond: to join together

cement: to glue together

crystal: a mineral that has shapes with flat surfaces and sharp edges

igneous rock: rock made from melted minerals

magma: melted rock inside Earth

metamorphic rock: rock that has been changed by heat and squeezing

mineral: a substance found in nature. Minerals are solid. They are not alive.

sediment: a bit of mud, sand, stone, shell, or bone

sedimentary rock: rock that forms when bits of mud, sand, stone, shell, or bone are glued together

streak plate: a tool for studying minerals. People scrape minerals across streak plates to see if the minerals make colored lines.

Learn More about Minerals

Books

Green, Dan. *Rocks and Minerals: A Gem of a Book!* New York: Kingfisher, 2009. Rocks and minerals introduce themselves to the reader in this funny and informative book.

Pellant, Chris. *Quartz and Other Minerals.* Milwaukee: Gareth Stevens, 2007. The mineral quartz takes center stage in this interesting title on minerals.

Tomecek, Steve. *Rocks & Minerals.* Washington, DC: National Geographic Society, 2010. Playful illustrations bring rocks and minerals to life.

Walker, Sally M. *Researching Rocks.* Minneapolis: Lerner Publications Company, 2013. If you liked what you learned about rocks in this book, then you'll love investigating rocks even more!

Websites

Enchanted Learning: Geology, Rocks, and Minerals
http://www.enchantedlearning.com/geology
This Enchanted Learning page is just the thing for budding Earth scientists.

Rocks for Kids
http://www.rocksforkids.com
This page talks about how rocks and minerals form, how to identify rocks and minerals, and how rocks and minerals are used.

Science News for Kids
http://www.sciencenewsforkids.org
This online magazine has articles all about science. It also has games, science fair news, and information on science experiments.

LERNER

SOURCE™

Expand learning beyond the printed book. Download free, complementary educational resources for this book from our website, www.lerneresource.com.

Index

Photo Acknowledgments

The images in this book are used with the permission of: © Flirt/SuperStock, p. 4; © John Cancalosi/age fotostock/SuperStock, p. 5; © Citi Jo/Shutterstock.com, p. 6; © Bertrand Rieger/Hemis/CORBIS, p. 7; © Mark Schneider/Visuals Unlimited, Inc., pp. 8, 19; © Albert Copley/Visuals Unlimited, Inc., p. 9, 23; © age fotostock/SuperStock, p. 10 (left); © Thomas Hunn/Visuals Unlimited, Inc., p. 10 (right); © Laura Westlund/Independent Picture Service, pp. 11, 18; © Jose Manuel Sanchis Calvete/CORBIS, p. 12; © Javier Trueba/MSF/Photo Researchers, Inc., p. 13; © Arnold Fisher/Photo Researchers, Inc., p. 14; © Visuals Unlimited/CORBIS, p. 15; © Dr. John D. Cunningham/Visuals Unlimited, Inc., p. 16; © Thomas Hunn/Visuals Unlimited, Inc., p. 17; © Charles D. Winters/Photo Researchers, Inc., p. 20; © Ken Lucas/Visuals Unlimited, Inc., p. 21; © Steve McCutcheon/Visuals Unlimited/CORBIS, p. 22; © iStockphoto.com/Drazen Vukelic, p. 24; © Artic-Images/Iconica/Getty Images, p. 25; © Scientifica/Visuals Unlimited/CORBIS, p. 26; © Scientifica/Visuals Unlimited, Inc., pp. 27, 28, 31; © Dirk Wiersma/Photo Researchers, Inc., p. 29; © Joyce Photographics/Photo Researchers, Inc., p. 30; © Todd Strand/Independent Picture Service, p. 32; © Apple Tree House/Riser/Getty Images, p. 33; © Adam Crowley/Photodisc/Getty Images, p. 34; © Comstock Images/Getty Images, p. 35; © Michele Cornelius/Dreamstime.com, p. 36; © Mark Schneider/Visuals Unlimited/CORBIS, p. 37.

Front cover: © Albert Copley/Visuals Unlimited, Inc.

Main body text set in Adrianna Regular 14/20.
Typeface provided by Chank.